Color Right
Dress Right

The Total Look

Color

Importance of color

Color is important; it affects how we feel and how people respond to us. Industries use stimulating colors to increase production, hospitals use soothing colors to enhance recuperation, advertisers employ eye-catching colors to entice us to buy their products.

Researchers have found that colors evoke certain responses. For instance, navy blue suggests authority. Red is exciting, stimulating; pink, sweet and gentle; orange is friendly, outgoing; yellow, sunny and cheerful. Green makes us feel tranquil and blue is also a soothing color. Purple is regal, dignified; brown, dependable; black is sophisticated and mysterious; white is innocent and gray is safe, comforting and protective.

So colors are important in creating the look we want to achieve and influencing other people's mental reactions to us. A navy suit teamed with a white shirt is especially authoritative and commands respect. Wearing various shades of the same color, especially the neutrals (black, gray, taupe, beige and cream), creates an elegant look; contrasting light and dark colors create a dramatic effect. Of course, a color can also have negative associations. For example, too much pink can be saccharine.

Obviously, not everyone responds to color in exactly the same way, but general responses are so well proved that they can be relied upon. According to John T. Molloy, author of *Dress for Success*, men are attracted to women wearing pale yellow, pale pink, navy, shades of blue, red and tan. They do not like mustard, chartreuse or lavender shades.

Women are instinctively attracted to the colors that most become them, but, unfortunately, they do not always select their most flattering colors because of the influence of parents, friends, sales people and childhood associations with color.

Women are also influenced by colors and styles currently in vogue. Each season designers show their new lines in particular colors, and fashion-conscious women are the first to wear them. But the latest colors may not always be the right ones for every woman. The right shades are those that accentuate the natural hair, skin, and eye coloring.

In recent years the Chinese and Japanese influence on fashion has resulted in a new simplicity – a rethinking of color and design. They use neutrals as important basic colors.

Color is the most important element in either enhancing your appearance or detracting from it. The easiest way to look your most attractive is to wear your best colors. If someone compliments you on the way you look, it probably means that the color you have chosen is right for you.

Selecting your colors

Three natural colors are the best guides for choosing the colors of your clothes and cosmetics. They are hair color, complexion color and eye color. Of these, the first, the original natural color of the hair, is the most important.

Hair colors fall into three general groups – brunette, the most common, blonde and redhead. To find the colors of clothes, cosmetics and accessories that suit you best, you should refer to the hair color group to which you belong.

If you are not quite sure about the color of your complexion, examine your forearm. Turn your hand palm-up and see whether the delicate skin between your wrist and elbow shows a pink, rose, olive, white, beige or brown tint. Compare this part of your arm to a friend's with a different coloring and you should see the difference between one type of complexion and another.

Brunettes
Women with medium-to-dark brown and black hair are included in this group. Brunette hair is associated with complexions that range from white-beige, beige with a hint of pink, golden beige and light or dark olive, to black (see below). Eye color is usually brown or hazel, speckled tones of gray or green, gray or deep blue.

There are two exceptions to this group. The first is the woman whose hair color was originally blonde (until she was about fifteen years old) but has darkened with age and is now medium-brown. She has a reddish complexion and belongs to the pale blonde group. In this case, eye color is usually green, hazel, blue, blue-green, or dark brown.

The other exception is the brunette who has definite auburn or red high-lights in her hair and has a reddish or copper complexion. She belongs in the redhead group. Her eyes are usually green, hazel or golden brown.

Although dark-skinned brunettes can wear essentially the same colors, there are exceptions, and so we have included them in a separate category. Here we discuss those women with dark brown, brown-black or black hair; skin color which ranges from light brown to mahogany to black; and hazel, gray, gray-green, dark brown or black eyes.

Blondes
The blonde group is subdivided into two categories – pale blondes and golden blondes. Pale blonde hair color can range from platinum and light blonde to brownish blonde. The pale blonde has ash tones in her hair, her complexion is usually pale or translucent and her eyes are light – light blue, light gray or blue-green. The golden blonde group ranges from light golden brown to strawberry blonde; no ash tones are visible in the hair. The golden blonde's complexion is peach or ivory and she has a tendency to blush easily. Her eye color is either crystal blue, blue with brown flecks, blue-green or golden-brown.

Redheads
The third hair color group consists of women with light red to dark auburn and brown hair with definite red or auburn tones. The complexion is usually fair or reddish, and eyes are turquoise, green, blue, brown or hazel.

The color wheel
Selecting pleasing color combinations can be difficult. However, by referring to the color wheel, we can see instantly the colors that look good together and those that provide the best contrasts.

The bright primary colors – blue, red and yellow – are the pure colors from which all other colors derive. They can make us feel vivacious and exciting. When equal amounts of blue and red are mixed together, a secondary color, violet, is created; mixing blue and yellow creates green; mixing yellow and red produces orange. This mixing creates complementary colors (the secondary colors opposite the primary colors that have *not* been used in their making). So, yellow and violet are complementary colors, as are green and red, and blue and orange. Complementary colors provide the greatest contrasts; when worn together they seem to bring out the best in each other.

The other colors in the wheel are made up of equal parts of a primary and its closest secondary. Any adjacent colors, such as yellow and light green, match in a subtle but pleasing way.

When we refer to cool colors, we mean those colors with blue tones in them – blue-red, blue-green, fuchsia, magenta and purple. Warm colors are colors with yellow or gold tones in them – yellow-orange, orange, or yellow-red, for example. We also refer to monochromatic color schemes. These are combinations in which lighter or darker shades of the same color are used, for instance, in the blue family, shades from pale aqua to dark blue-green.

The neutrals include black, white, off-white, most of the browns from beige to dark brown through camel and nutmeg, and grays from pale silver to charcoal.

We have employed the color wheel principle in creating the wardrobe color combinations and in the color charts attached inside the front cover. Although we have already done the work for you, you might like to refer to the wheel to make up your own combinations. Be sure to choose those shades from the color range suitable to your particular hair and skin coloring, as described in the following chapters.

Your best colors
We have selected a range of colors which is the most suitable for the clothes, accessories and cosmetics for each hair color group. Some of the colors are core colors – you can build an entire wardrobe around them.

Others are more suitable as accent colors – used in smaller articles of clothing, accessories or cosmetics.

To help you use your best colors to create an effective but economical wardrobe, we have provided several sets of three-color combinations in each hair group (see pp. 69-73). They should simplify your shopping for clothes and accessories, help eliminate costly mistakes and take the guess-work out of mixing and matching separate articles.

Color charts
For your convenience, we've enclosed color charts in the inside cover for each particular skin and hair type. Remove the chart showing the colors for your type and keep it in your hand-bag for use as a guide when you shop for clothes, cosmetics and accessories. The chart will serve as a reminder for choosing colors, say, in matching a belt to a suit or a lipstick to a dress; it will enable you to select a wardrobe in which absolutely everything is color-co-ordinated. In the long term, you'll economize by choosing only those colors that suit you, and any "look" you wear will be a "total" look.

The color wheel can be an inspiration in creating combinations that work well together.

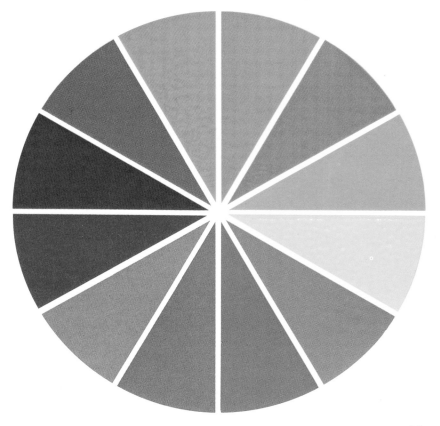

11

Brunettes

Hair color:
Medium-to-dark brown, black or jet-black

Complexion:
White-beige, beige with a hint of pink, golden beige (Oriental skin tones), or light or dark olive

Eye color:
Brown, hazel, speckled tones of gray or green, gray or deep blue

Rows of bright red poppies, clusters of white orchids, and sprigs of violets provide you with the right background.

Your best colors are from the palette of the artist Mondrian: black, white, red and blue.

Cool colors are the colors for you — those that have blue undertones, such as deep red, green, and blue-green. Pure white is especially flattering against your dark hair color, as are the white-based tones of frosty pink, blue, mint and lemon.

Clear and vivid colors make you look outstanding. You can wear combinations of sharply contrasting colors such as black and white, red and white and red and black as well as blue and black, navy and burgundy and orchid and green.

Warm colors, colors that have yellow or gold added, are to be avoided: gold, orange, ginger, brown, red with a yellow cast, green with a yellow cast and rust. Soft pastels, also, are not flattering for you.

● Brunettes with olive skin look particularly attractive in white, navy or magenta.

● Fair skins appear more vivacious in bright shades of emerald, purple and red. Off-white is preferable to pure white as this can be harsh against very fair skin.

● Oriental skins glow in magenta, purple and poppy red.

Altered hair color

True brunettes never look their best as blondes. Nevertheless, should you decide to dye your hair blonde, make sure that the color is in ash tones. Never use warm, red or golden tones. The same is true of highlights — ash tones will give a much lighter look and flatter your complexion.

Jet-black hair is the most flattering for Oriental skin tones and coloring your hair red or blonde is not recommended.

Brunettes tend to gray prematurely, and the gray usually becomes a clear silver white. Gray hair can be left natural, or highlighted with a rinse. If you wish to cover the gray, dye it a shade or two lighter than your original hair color.

Brunette types

**Brown-black hair
Pinky-beige complexion
Blue eyes**

**Jet-black hair
White-beige complexion
Hazel eyes**

**Silver-gray hair
Beige complexion
Gray-blue eyes**

**Medium-brown hair
Light olive complexion
Brown eyes**

Your color chart

The 24 colors below were selected especially for brunettes who look stunning in cool, blue-based tones. The first ten colors are your core colors. Any one of these is appropriate for all the basic items in your wardrobe — coats, suits, skirts and pants. The neutral shades are also the most suitable for accessories. The remaining colors are more adaptable as accent colors for smaller items such as sweaters, blouses and scarves. On the following pages we recommend shades of these colors for choosing cosmetics, accessories and jewelry, and we suggest wardrobe color combinations on p. 72.

You can carry your colors everywhere by taking your color chart to use as a shopping guide.

Your core colors

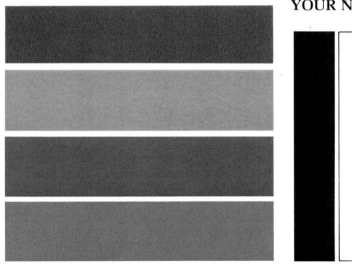

YOUR NEUTRALS

Your accent colors

16

Your color chart

Generally, all brunettes can wear the same basic colors. However, brunettes with darker skins should go for the very bold colors (brilliant red, stark white, bright blue, hot pink) which will bring out the rich amber tones of your complexions.

The first ten colors are your core colors. Any one of these is appropriate for all the basic items in your wardrobe – coats, suits, skirts and pants. The neutral shades are also the most suitable for accessories. The remaining colors are more adaptable as accent colors for smaller items such as sweaters, blouses and scarves.

On the following pages we recommend shades of these colors for choosing cosmetics, accessories and jewelry, and we suggest wardrobe color combinations on p. 73.

You can carry your colors everywhere by taking your color chart to use as a shopping guide.

Your core colors

YOUR NEUTRALS

Your accent colors

Your best colors

Below are the right colors for your cosmetics and accessories. They reflect the colors we have set down for you on the previous page. Always think about the three or four colors in your wardrobe (see p. 73) and choose the "extras" to match them.

When you go shopping, take along your color chart to help you choose a neutral handbag or a bright lipstick that will co-ordinate with your clothes. You will soon achieve a total look in which everything works together.

COSMETICS

Foundation   Amber, dark honey, copper-tan, beige-tan. Light or dark cover stick

Blusher   Bright red, plum, orchid, amber-rose, pink or red cheek gloss

Eye shadow   Shades of rose, plum, teal, mid-to-navy blue, smokey violet, taupe, blue-black

Eye liner   Electric blue, mauve, soft brown-black

Mascara   Brown-black, purple

Lipstick   Rose-red, brilliant red, plum, raspberry, mocha-red lipstick or gloss

Lip pencil   Plum, light brown

Nail polish   Red, plum, fuchsia

ACCESSORIES

Glasses   If you wear glasses, you can wear more eye color. Rose tones and smokey gray-violet eye shadows create an attractive combination under clear-toned glasses. You can select thin red wire frames, gray, silver or clear frames

Jewelry   Diamanté in blue, pink or clear colors; ivory, onyx, garnet, sapphire, white pearls. Select rings, chains and earrings in silver or a combination of silver and gold

Shoes & handbags   Black and taupe; white and red for summer; silver for cocktail or evening wear

Hosiery   Slate gray, black, suntan shades; cobalt blue or red can be worn in thicker ribbed stockings

Colors in action

This woman's large round eyes are one of her best features. However, her patchy (light and dark) skin tone, high forehead and a bottom lip that is lighter in color than the top all make her a prime candidate for a color make-over.

Day

A dark concealer evens out her patchy skin and a bronze foundation gives all-over color. Amber translucent powder makes the skin glow. Contouring in brown-toned blusher softens her square chin. A raspberry blusher on the cheekbones and temples and highlighter above the blusher (towards the hairline) create high cheekbones. Her eyes come to life with charcoal shadow on corners, brick on corners of brow bones and plum blended with charcoal on lids. A lip toner in her own lip color matches bottom lip to top; plum lip pencil with light plum lipstick and a frosted gloss completes this sophisticated, professional look

Evening

An exciting party mood is achieved with vivid color, shine and sparkle. Here a coppery tan foundation creates a richer, more shimmering look. Iridescent powder under the brow bone highlights and accents the eyes. Coal-black and midnight blue eye shadows are applied with a wet brush to outline the eyes and applied dry (and heavily) to the lids and corners and smudged. Both black and electric blue mascaras are stroked onto lashes to give them deep color. Soft brown pencil outlines and shapes the lips and magenta frosted lipstick flashes color. Bangs sprinkled with glitter will make her shimmer by night.

This young woman, too, has problems common to many dark-skinned brunettes – her complexion is uneven, with dark tones around her nostrils and shadows under the eyes, and her bottom lip is lighter in color than her top lip. Also, her hair is straggly and unkempt; her heart-shaped face should be elongated by careful contouring.

Day

We applied concealer to block-out the shadows around her eyes, nostrils and laugh-lines. Copper and tan foundation colors are blended together to correct the unven tone of her skin. Lip toner in a natural brown color matches her bottom lip to her top lip; fuchsia lipstick is applied over this. Violet and mauve eye shadows blended on the lids, black kohl pencil and black mascara add depth to her captivating eyes. A mauve-pink blusher is placed in the middle of her high cheekbones, making the cheeks look more hollow, and above the temples and along the hairline, to make the widest part of her face appear more narrow

Evening

A copper glow foundation and pearlized, loose powder set her make-up. Tawny gold eye shadow is blended with plum towards the corner of the eyes and a beige highlighter applied to the brow bone. Soft blue-black pencil lines extend from the bottom lid towards the brow to create a winged look. Brown-black mascara is applied heavily, creating fuller lashes and emphasizing her almond-shaped eyes. Bright magenta-pink lipstick with a light glimmer of clear lip gloss on the bottom lip make her face sparkle. Pinky-red powder blush on the temples creates a soft effect and red cheek gloss adds a radiant glow to complete her evening look

Pale blondes

Hair color:
Platinum, flaxen blonde, dark blonde, brown (once blonde) – all with natural ash tones

Complexion:
Pale or translucent, reddish

Eye color:
Light blue, light gray, hazel, blue or blue-green

Cherry blossoms, lilac bushes and tea roses of pink, white and pale lemon are your best setting. Your colors are the soft blues and pinhs in the paintings of Monet and the gray-blues and pale sunlight yellows in the changing skies of Turner. Pastel shades of sugared almonds, watermelons, raspberries and cherries complement your delicate coloring. The neutrals ranging from off-white to taupe, rose-brown and camel are most becoming to you. Avoid stark white, rich golds, orange tones and olive green.
- If you have ash blonde or cream-colored hair, a pale translucent complexion and blue eyes, soft pink and clear blue colors are flattering.
- The blonde whose hair has turned darker with age looks good in blue-gray, burgundy and bright pink.
- The brunette (once blonde, with a ruddy tone to her complexion) looks especially attractive in blue-red, pink-red, camel, taupe and purple.

Altered hair color
Most blonde hair colors go gray elegantly into a lustrous shade of silver. If, however, you wish to tint your hair another color or return to your natural color, use ash blonde or ash brown tones. Avoid red or gold shades. A particularly pleasing effect is an ash brown base with highlights of light-ened blonde. This gives a very natural look and is softer than a solid blonde.

Pale blonde types

Flaxen hair
Pale, translucent complexion
Gray-blue eyes

Darkened blonde hair
Pinky-beige complexion
Teal blue eyes

Brown (once blonde) hair
Ruddy complexion
Light blue eyes

Your color chart

The soft shades below are the ones that complement your delicate complexion.

The first ten colors are your core colors. Any one of these is appropriate for all the basic items in your wardrobe – coats, suits, skirts and pants. The neutral shades are also the most suitable for accessories. The remaining colors are more adaptable as accent colors for smaller items such as sweaters, blouses and scarves.

On the following pages we recommend shades of these colors for choosing cosmetics, accessories and jewelry, and we suggest wardrobe color combinations on p. 70.

You can carry your colors everywhere by taking your color chart to use as a shopping guide.

Your core colors

YOUR NEUTRALS

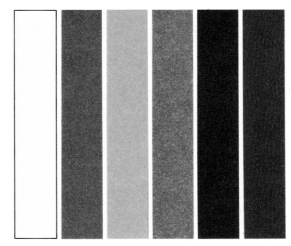

Your accent colors

Golden blondes

Hair color:
Light golden brown, Scandinavian blonde, strawberry blonde — all with natural golden tones

Complexion:
Peach or ivory; many have a tendency to blush easily

Eye color:
Crystal blue, blue with brown flecks, blue-green or golden brown

Fields of cornflowers, daffodils and budding crocuses create the right background for the "golden girl". The palette of David Hockney, with its bright blues, golds, yellows and corals, is what flatters you most. Warm colors, that is, colors warmed with gold, are for you. Your best colors are the subtle shades of cream, ivory, peach and camel, the bright gold of the Californian sun and a clear Mediterranean blue. Ivory, cream, tan and soft brown blend beautifully with the golden shades of your hair, creating a monochromatic, all-in-one look which is chic and elegant.

● All golden blondes should avoid fuchsia, burgundy, magenta, white and dark gray. Black and pure white look good only on suntanned skin and could be eliminated from your wardrobe completely. Navy and cream are good colors to use as substitutes, especially for accessories.
● Golden blondes with peachy-beige complexions and blue eyes look particularly good in bright blue and coral tones.
● Ivory and ivory-peach complexions are enhanced by the softer shades of peach, sand and yellow-green.
● The darker golden blonde with more color to her complexion is suited to the brighter corals, cornflower blues, golds and rusts.

Altered hair color

The combination of warm golden hair and a glowing complexion creates a bright, vivacious young look. But when your hair turns gray, consider dying it to its natural golden tone or golden brown. Or, leave your hair gray and highlight it with gold. Golden highlights can be very becoming on a light brown base, too.

Golden blonde types

Strawberry blonde hair
Pinky-peach complexion
Blue-green eyes

Tawny-gold hair
Creamy peach complexion
Turquoise-blue eyes

Darkened blonde hair
Golden-beige complexion
Hazel eyes

38

Your color chart

The 24 shades below are best for the woman with the peaches-and-cream complexion.

The first ten colors are your core colors. Any one of these is appropriate for all the basic items in your wardrobe – coats, suits, skirts and pants. The neutral shades are also the most suitable for accessories. The remaining colors are more adaptable as accent colors for smaller items such as sweaters, blouses and scarves.

On the following pages we recommend shades of these colors for choosing cosmetics, accessories and jewelry, and we suggest wardrobe color combinations on p. 71.

You can carry your colors everywhere by taking your color chart to use as a shopping guide.

Your core colors

YOUR NEUTRALS

Your accent colors

Your best colors

Below are the right colors for your cosmetics and accessories. They reflect the colors we have set down for you on the previous page. Always think about the three or four colors in your wardrobe (see p. 71) and choose the "extras" to match them. When you go shopping, take along your color chart to help you choose a neutral handbag or a bright lipstick that will co-ordinate with your clothes. You will soon achieve a total look in which everything – clothes, cosmetics and accessories – works together.

COSMETICS

Foundation   Ivory to peach tones, warm beige, mocha, tan

Blusher   Peach, coral, ginger

Eye shadow   Smudgy brown, russet, golden tones, aqua tints and smokey blue to violet

Eye liner   Smudgy brown, smokey blue

Mascara   Brown, electric blue

Lipstick   Peach, pinky coral, ginger-brown, mocha, orange-red

Lip pencil   Orange-red, ginger, mocha

Nail polish   Shell peach, coral, mocha

ACCESSORIES

Glasses   If you wear glasses, you can wear more eye color. Rose-peach eye shadow tones combined with soft browns, blues or greens are flattering. Frames in natural flesh tones with rose-tinted lenses close to your skin color, or soft brown lenses in tan or brown frames, suit you best. Gold frames blend well with your hair color

Jewelry   Ivory, tiger's eye, amber, coral, topaz, turquoise, sapphire, black opal, creamy pearls, yellow diamonds

Shoes & handbags   Beige, tan, camel, navy

Hosiery   Beige, flesh tone, suntan and golden shades, gray-beige, navy

Colors in action

This blonde's beautiful natural hair shades of yellow and gold and her piercing blue eyes are her most striking features. She does have some redness on her nose and cheeks, however, and faint circles under her wide-set eyes. She also has a wide jaw, and her eyebrows need shaping.

Day

Green primer is applied to red areas to even-out the skin tone. Concealer eliminates the circles under her eyes, and golden-tan foundation blends in well with this woman's natural coloring. Golden peach eye shadow on the eyelids, mushroom color on the inner and outer corners, and a fine line of soft brown along the lower lashes seem to bring her eyes closer together. To soften our model's square jaw, tawny blusher is used on the cheeks, with a highlighter just above the blusher to create the illusion of high cheekbones; darker blusher is placed along the jawline. A shell-peach tint gives a natural sheen to the lips

Evening

From daytime elegance to night-time charm – a sparkling evening look is achieved with deeper eye and lip colors. Turquoise and aquamarine eye shadows are subtly blended on the lids; a thin line of deep blue eyeliner under the bottom lashes becomes heavier towards the corners, giving more shape and definition to the eyes. Mascara, applied heavily to the top and bottom corner lashes, adds depth to her piercing blue eyes. Soft coral blusher gives this model a warm, radiant glow, and her lips, lined in russet pencil, filled-in with copper lipstick and topped with a lustrous gloss, complete her gleaming after dark look

Like many golden blondes, this young woman has a florid, uneven coloring which needs toning-down. She has pretty, almond-shaped eyes, but her lashes are very light in color. Her lips are not well-defined and could benefit from a proper shaping.

Day

A pure, home-spun quality is reflected in our model's new day-time look. Green primer is used to tone down the red areas around her nose and concealer is applied to the circles under her eyes. A peach liquid tint also eliminates the redness in her complexion and brick cream blusher along the cheekbones complement her coloring. Beige highlighter is applied along the brow bone and brown eye shadow on the inner corners of the lids. These plus smokey-brown pencil winging out from the bottom lashes and blending with green shadow make enchanting eyes. Ginger lipstick adds a soft touch to this lovely sunny look

Evening

Calm and old-fashioned by day, tantalizing temptress by night! Alluring eyes and sensuous lips are the crowning glory of this bewitching evening look. Soft blue eye shadow on the lid gives way to beige and brown, with gold highlighter smoothed on along the brow bone. Brown eye shadow also extends from the inside corner of the brow towards the bridge of the nose to give the nose a more defined look. The lashes are darkened dramatically by several coats of mascara. Apricot blusher and soft coral lipstick lend a luxurious, velvety finish. The hair is swept up off the shoulder creating more attention to the face

43

Redheads

Hair color:
Light red to dark auburn, and brown hair with definite red or auburn highlights

Complexion:
Fair or reddish, copper-toned

Eye color:
Turquoise, green or blue, golden brown

Vibrant flowers like tiger lilies, chrysanthymums and marigolds are those which best complement your exciting hair. Your best colors are those seen in paintings by Gauguin – lush greens, rich oranges, smudgy olives, terracotta. Redheads are fortunate because most designers use a wide selection of these colors, especially in the autumn.

Because your red hair is and should be the focus of attention, do not wear more than three colors at one time. One of the colors should blend with your hair: cinnamon, salmon or brick red. To achieve a more striking look, the second color should be the color of your eyes; if you have blue eyes use teal or aqua. A good three-color combination for a brown-eyed auburn-redhead is brick red, cream and chocolate (for more combinations, see redhead wardrobe colors, p. 69). All redheads should avoid fuchsia, unless a harsh, brashy effect is desired. Pink, plum and black are not in the redhead's color scheme at all.

● Redheads with fair or light, freckled pink complexions look best in softer shades – light beige, tan, salmon, olive and moss green – because very bright colors can be overwhelming.
● Redheads with copper skin look best in brighter colors, especially pumpkin, cinnamon-brown, brick, copper, topaz and bronze.
● Those light redheads whose hair color is a cross between strawberry blonde and light carrot-red, and whose complexions are whitish-pink, can borrow some of the clearer colors of the golden blonde – coral, sand, aqua and Mediterranean blue.
● Brick red is an exciting color for all redheads, and is very effective when combined with a neutral color such as beige or bone.

Altered hair color
Redheads do not gray attractively; the gray turns a tea color and yellows with age. We recommend coloring the hair. Our rule for redheads is: as you grow older, go lighter.

If you use henna, use a red or gold shade, colors with warm tones. If you dye your hair, avoid any cool or ash tones. You are best in golden colors, from strawberry to golden blonde and auburn. Delicate gold highlights in red hair look attractive and natural, as if highlighted by the sun. Applying lowlights is particularly effective for auburn hair – that is, using a red color just a shade or two lighter than your own. This results in a more subtle look than that of highlighting.

Redhead types

Brown hair (gold-red highlights)
Golden copper complexion
Green eyes

Dark auburn hair
Light peach complexion
Teal blue eyes

Auburn hair
Copper complexion
Topaz-colored eyes

Dark carrot-red hair
Peach freckled complexion
Amber-colored eyes

Your color chart

Although your best colors are those of the autumn leaves – bright orange, brick red, ginger-brown – the 24 shades below will help you look great in any season.

The first ten colors are your core colors. Any one of these is appropriate for all the basic items in your wardrobe – coats, suits, skirts and pants. The neutral shades are also the most suitable for accessories. The remaining colors are more adaptable as accent colors for smaller items such as sweaters, blouses and scarves.

On the following pages we recommend shades of these colors for choosing cosmetics, accessories and jewelry, and we suggest wardrobe color combinations on p. 69.

You can carry your colors everywhere by taking your color chart to use as a shopping guide.

Your core colors

YOUR NEUTRALS

Your accent colors

Your best colors

Below are the right colors for your cosmetics and accessories. They reflect the colors we have set down for you on the previous page. Always think about the three or four colors in your wardrobe (see p. 69) and choose the "extras" to match them. When you go shopping, take along your color chart to help you choose a neutral handbag or a bright lipstick that will co-ordinate with your clothes. You will soon achieve a total look in which everything – clothes, cosmetics and accessories – works together.

COSMETICS

Foundation   Golden beige, cream-beige, peach-beige

Blusher   Tawny, peach, apricot, coral

Eye shadow   Sludge green, russet, teal, golden copper

Eye liner   Moss green, charcoal, brown

Mascara   Dark brown, green

Lipstick   Brick red, coral, peach

Lip pencil   Light brown

Nail polish   Coral, brick red

ACCESSORIES

Hosiery   Flesh tone, bone, tan, gray-beige, olive. Avoid pink

Shoes & handbags   Bone, tan, brown, olive

Glasses   If you wear glasses you can wear more eye color. For green eyes, use teal and soft brown shadows; for golden brown eyes, ginger or copper; for brown eyes, teal or turquoise. If you wear tinted glasses, your lens color should be in golden amber, peach or smokey brown tones. Tan, camel, russet-red or tortoise-shell frames suit you, as do gold, amber or skin-toned frames. Avoid pink, pale blue and red frames. Metal and clear plastic are not flattering either

Jewelry   Ivory, wood, coral, amber, tiger's eye, jade, turquoise, emerald, topaz, yellow diamonds, pearls with a yellow cast

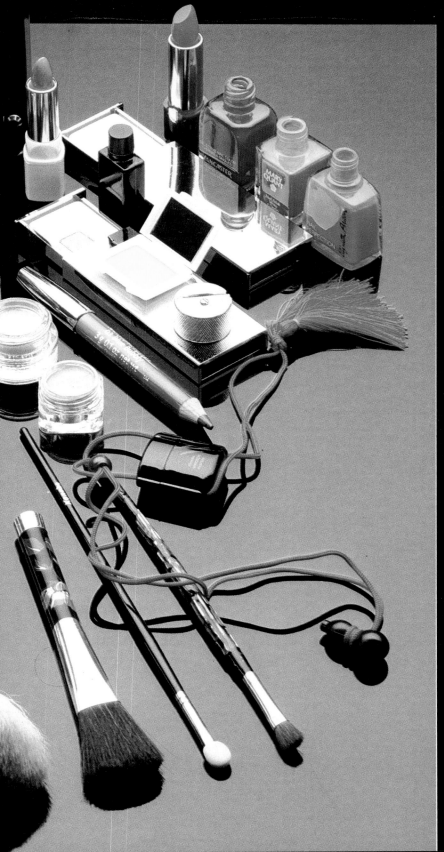

come in various shades, so choose one that matches your skin type. Translucent powder can be used for all types of skin; it has no color and will not change the shade of the foundation. To give an all-over luminous look, use iridescent or pearlized powder.

Blusher, or rouge, comes in powder, cream or liquid form and is applied with a brush, a damp sponge or your fingertips. It should harmonize with your lipstick color and skin toner. The lighter your skin, the lighter your blusher should be.

Eyebrow pencils can help you create a more expressive face, as you use them to reshape your eyebrows. You will need two pencils, one in your natural hair color and the other a shade lighter for highlighting. The combination of these colors will give a more natural look.

Eye shadow comes in several forms: pressed powder, loose powder, cream stick and liquid cream. Choose whichever you are most comfortable with. The color needn't match your eye tone, but make sure that it does not overpower your natural eye color.

Eye liner makes the lashes appear fuller, but it should be applied subtly. Use either a pencil or a fine-tipped sable brush. Neutral smoky shades such as charcoal, gray and brown give the most natural look.

Mascara accentuates the eyes and gives them depth and dimension. It comes in cake or cream form and can be applied with brushes, wands or combs.

Lipstick comes in sticks, creams, and glosses, as tubes or in pots. Outlining your lips with a lip brush or pencil will help you follow your natural lip line smoothly and accurately and results in a clean, neat look.

MAKING-UP

1. **Foundation** *Place a large dot on forehead, cheeks and chin and blend with a damp sponge so there is no distinct line between face and neck. Apply also over eyelids and lips so shadow and lipstick will last longer.*

2. **Concealer** *Gently pat on three dots under lower lash line and blend outwards and around outer corner of eye only.*

3. **Powder** *Dip brush in loose, translucent powder, shake off any excess, and brush lightly all over face, including eyelids and lips.*

4. **Blusher** *Apply from the cheekbones upwards to the temples. The intensity of the color should lessen gradually outwards towards your ears so that it does not end abruptly at your hairline.*

5. **Eye make-up** *Pencil most brow hairs in your base color, with scattered strokes in your highlight color. Make light, feathery strokes, one hair at a time, in the same direction of the brow. Start at inner corner of brow and work outwards. Blend shadows well so color changes from eye to brow are gradual. Line the lids with eye liner. Use a fine spiral mascara brush to curl your lashes as you add color.*

6. **Lipstick** *Outline lips with pencil in the same shade as your lipstick or a shade darker. Fill in with lipstick.*

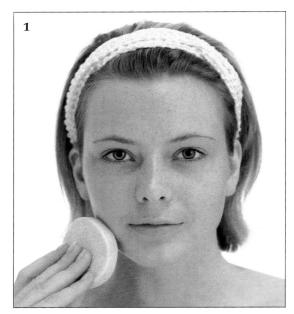

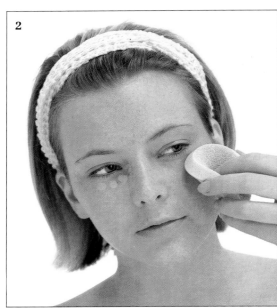

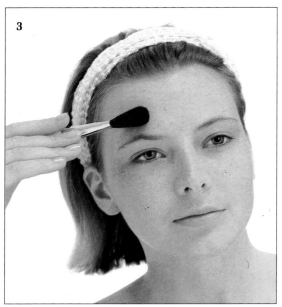

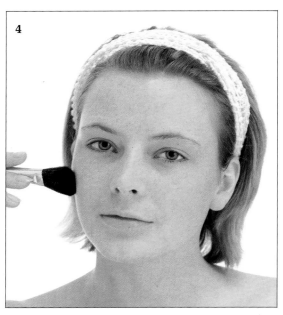

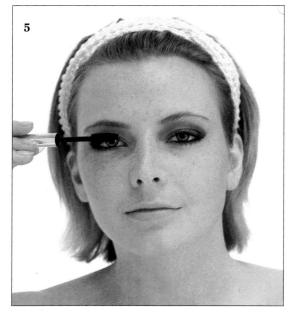

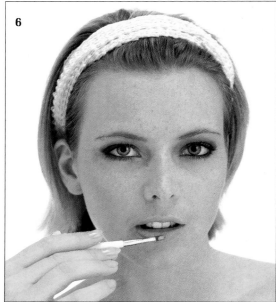

Creative cosmetics

Cosmetics, when applied properly, can not only highlight your positive features, but can minimize negative ones. They can create larger eyes or fuller lips, draw attention away from a crooked nose, and even change the shape of your face.

THE EYES

Your eyes are probably the most expressive part of your face. Do not despair if they aren't your best feature – there is something you can do to make them more attractive if you follow the advice set out below.

If you have protruding eyes:
Outline the shape of your eyes with eyeliner close to the upper and lower lashes. Use dark shadow on the lid up to the brow bone and apply highlighter directly under the brow. Emphasize the top lashes by curling them, and apply two coats of mascara.

If you have deep-set eyes:
Draw a thin line of frosted shadow along the top lashes. Apply a light frosted shadow over the lids to "bring them out" and a deeper shadow on the brow bone. Use a lighter-colored liner on the inner corner of the upper lid. Outline the corners of your eyes, from the center outwards. Apply mascara heavily to outer-corner lashes.

If you have hooded eyes:
Fill in the complete area between the upper lashes and the eyebrow with a medium-toned eye shadow (gray, for instance). Apply a deeper tone of the same shade (gray-blue), which is the contour color, diagonally from the center of the lid to the outer corner of the eyebrow. Use a deep colored pencil or brush from the center of the lower lid towards the outer corner of the eye, almost to the brow. This line should be very thin and it should be smudged in the outer corner.

If you have small eyes:
Apply a light frosted shadow around the entire eye. Blend well so that it is almost unnoticeable. Blend one or two darker shadows on the lid, the crease of the eye and under the bottom lashes. Use a highlighter on the inner half of the brow bone and draw a thin pencil line to the upper and lower corner lashes. Apply mascara.

THE LIPS

People often look at your mouth when you speak, so make your lips as nice as possible by shaping them correctly.

If you have thin lips:
Use lighter shades of lipstick to make your lips seem larger. Line your lips with a lip pencil, extending the line a little above your top lip and a little below your bottom lip. Make sure to extend it well into the corners. Using two shades of lipstick with the darker shade applied in the corners and the lighter towards the center of the lips gives the impression of a fuller mouth.

If you have full lips:
Apply foundation over lips. Use a soft lip pencil slightly darker than the lip color you intend to wear and draw a line slightly inside your natural lip line. Draw the line from the outer corner to the inner, resting your little finger on your chin to steady your hand. Use two shades of lipstick – one light applied to the outer corners of your mouth, and one dark to fill in the center.

If you have a wide mouth:
Avoid very bright colors of lipstick. Apply foundation on the outside corners of the mouth. Follow your natural lip line with a lip pencil, keeping a little inside it. Apply a dark shade of lipstick more heavily in the center of your lips; taper off and use a lighter color at the corners. Curve the upper lip slightly at the ends.

Facial shapes

As the saying goes, "Your face is your fortune". Unhappily, not everyone is so fortunate as to have a perfectly-shaped face. The basic facial shapes are oval, round, square, long and thin, and heart-shaped. The oval face is generally considered to be the most desirable shape; the bone structure is balanced, and no cosmetic correction is needed.

Contouring, coloring and highlighting with cosmetics can change the shape of your face dramatically. Round faces can be slimmed down and square faces can be made to look more oval. Double chins can be made to look less prominent and long chins shorter.

Contouring is shading the face with a brown-toned blusher to create shadows which can, among other things, make the cheeks look more "hollow", the nose more aquiline or the chin less obvious.

Coloring is adding color with either pink, peach or red-toned blusher to make the face look more alive. Applied in upward-and-outward strokes, coloring can give the face a "lift", creating a healthy youthful appearance.

Highlighting is applying a light or frosted powder on cheek, eye or lip areas to focus attention to a particular spot. By highlighting, you can create high cheekbones, larger eyes or moist-looking, sensuous lips.

Determining facial shape

Pin your hair back completely off your face. Look into a large mirror at arm's length, close one eye and trace your face in the mirror with a piece of soap or washable crayon. If the shape of your face is other than the desirable oval, you can create the illusion of a more oval shape by contouring, coloring and highlighting, see below.

If your face is round:
Create hollows in your cheeks by applying brown-toned blusher in a wide triangle, its base at the outer part of the face, its apex inward. Start at the upper tip of the ear, slant down towards the middle of the face, then towards the jawline. Apply a small triangle of

56

color blusher above the contour with its apex towards the eye. Highlighter should be applied from the outer corner of the eye towards the blush area on cheek.

If your face is square:
Apply a triangle of color blusher lower than you would for a round face, with its apex coming in towards the nose and the wide part extending toward the jawline. This creates a more hollow look and minimizes the width of the jaw. Highlighter placed just above the blusher accentuates your cheek-bones, making them appear higher.

If your face is long and thin:
Place your color blusher high on the cheeks, stroking horizontally. Avoid putting color under the cheekbones. Apply highlighter to the outer corners of the eyes towards the blusher on your cheeks. This emphasizes the horizontal line, creating a wider look. To "shorten" a long chin, apply brown-toned blusher to the chin area.

If your face is heart-shaped:
Place squares of color blusher in the middle of your high cheekbones, making the cheeks look more hollow. Highlighter should be applied subtly to the middle of the squares of blusher to bring attention to the center of your face. Contouring with brown-toned blusher above the temples and along the hairline can make the widest part of your face look narrower.

Make-up hints:
● *To give the illusion of a slimmer jawline or eliminate a "double chin", apply a brown-toned blusher just under the jawbone from ear to ear and blend up towards the middle of the face.*
● *To give your face a brighter look when you are tired, apply some color to your chin, forehead and cheeks.*
● *Blusher should be kept towards the outside of the face, never coming closer to the middle of the face than just below the middle of the eye. If you blend it near your nose, it will make your nose look heavier; if you apply it around your eyes, it will emphasize the circles.*

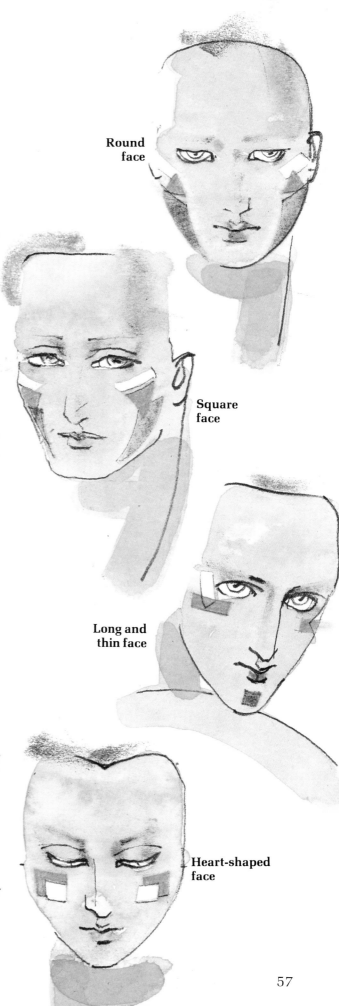

Round face

Square face

Long and thin face

Heart-shaped face

57

Hair

Beauty begins with the hair. If your hair doesn't look right, your total look will be wrong. To look its best, your hair must be clean. Frequent shampooing is not damaging to the hair, provided you choose a shampoo that is specially formulated for your hair type.

Shampoos

Shampoo for normal hair will clean hair without drying it. Shampoo for oily hair will remove excess oil. Shampoo for damaged hair is extra-gentle. When you shampoo, work suds into the scalp first, then through your hair, massaging gently with your fingertips (not nails). A lot of lather is not necessary; neither is more than one washing unless you have very oily hair. Use warm, not hot, water and rinse well. A final rinse with cool water gives the hair more shine.

Conditioners

Conditioners work wonders for the hair. They prevent and repair damage to the hair, add body to thin hair and make hair easier to comb and style. Conditioners are applied after shampooing and rinsing. Remember that they are formulated for the hair, not the scalp, and work best on the ends.

There are two types of conditioners: instant conditioners which are left on the hair for a few minutes, and penetrating conditioners which remain on the hair for 15–30 minutes. The penetrating conditioners work best for "problem" hair.

Damaged hair

Excessive heat from hair dryers, electric rollers or curling irons and chemically-induced changes to the hair such as coloring, straightening or permanent waves, may cause breaking, split ends, and dryness. But don't despair if your hair is damaged – there are several things you can do to revitalize it:

● Cut the split ends often, and get a style that requires as little setting as possible. Try to let your hair dry naturally.

● Massage your scalp gently to stimulate the oil glands.

● Use a hot oil treatment or a penetrating conditioner every two weeks.

● Use a wide-toothed comb and a soft-bristled brush.

● To give your hair a shinier, healthier look, use a cream "thickener" and let it remain on your hair between shampoos. Thickeners contain proteins and oils that coat the hair with an invisible film, making the hair thicker and giving the illusion of more volume. For best results, it should be applied after every shampoo.

Coloring your hair

The key to choosing the right hair color is knowing what is harmonious with your natural coloring. Redheads look most effective when warm golden glints or red tones are added to their hair. Most blondes look attractive with subtle highlights, which can give them a chic, expensive look. Medium-to-dark brown hair color is most suitable for olive, sallow, ruddy-skinned or dark-skinned brunettes; warm red tones are not. Brunettes with fair or white complexions should choose ash-brown, dark brown or brown-black shades. Those determined to go blonde should consider beige-blonde or ash-blonde highlights framing the face rather than an all-over color. This creates a softer, younger-looking effect.

Changing your hair color can make a dramatic change in your looks. For the best results go to a professional. We recommend that the permanent colorings – highlighting and low-lighting, tinting and bleaching – be applied only by a hairdresser. However, the hair coloring products which are often used at home with little difficulty are: shampoo and henna rinses, colored gels and mousses. Always test a home coloring product for allergic reaction before using it on your entire head and read all the instructions carefully.

Shampoo rinses are left on the hair after regular shampooing, then rinsed out. Depending on the product, this temporary color can last anywhere between one and six shampoos.

Gels and mousses are used for styling and conditioning, as well as temporary coloring. They can be massaged into wet or dry hair and either finger-dried or blow-dried. Both gels and mousses add a subtle all-over color to the hair.

Henna is a natural dye which is mainly used to give an all-over reddish tint. It comes as a powder, which is mixed with hot water to form a paste and applied to damp hair. Being a natural coloring, henna does not damage hair. However, it should not be used on fair hair or gray hair, as it may result in a bright orange color.

Highlighting is applying permanent dye to selected strands of hair, giving a soft effect of added color. A perforated rubber cap is placed tightly on the head and fine strands are pulled through the holes. A color solution is then applied to the strands. Some salons add highlights by sectioning strands separately from the rest of the hair and wrapping them in silver foil, leaving them until the desired color is reached.

Lowlighting is a very subtle way of brightening the hair. Shades of the same color are subtly blended to add rich color tones to your natural hair color. It is usually applied to brown hair to give reddish-brown lights.

Tinting makes the original hair color lighter or darker by up to four shades. It can be very effective on all types of hair and is often used to cover gray.

Bleaching is a strong permanent chemical method – it can make hair as light as you want. A paste is painted onto the roots and through the ends of the hair. Bleach contains both ammonia and peroxide, which are damaging to the hair, so deep conditioning treatments (the best are given by professionals) should be used to keep hair healthy.

HAIR STYLES
The right color, the right cut, the right styling – these are the elements for making the most of your hair.

Just as cosmetics are effective in changing the shape of your face, so are different hair styles.

To change the look of a square face, you need to draw attention away from the jaw. Get plenty of fullness on top of your head – wearing hair off the forehead elongates the face, and wisps of hair near the jawbone softens the harsh square look.

If you have a round face, cutting your hair close to the nape of your neck makes your neck, and consequently your face, appear longer; more volume on top also lengthens the face and asymmetrical bangs create a narrowing illusion. Short, blunt-cut hair sweeping upwards draws the eye "up" and adds length to a round face.

The temples and forehead of a heart-shaped face benefit by the softening effect brought on by short hair which is brushed back into a sleek wave. The layered bob "cuts" into the widest part of the jaw, giving a narrower appearance.

A long face needs a lot of fullness on the sides for balance, especially if the chin is rather narrow, like our model's. A thick headband flattens the crown of the head and shortens the face.

Square Face

Round Face

Heart-shaped Face

Long Face

61

Figure types

The advertising media have created an ideal woman – she has perfect proportions and a complete lack of figure faults. She is usually five or six inches taller than the average woman, and much slimmer.

Few of us fall into this perfect mould – short women want to look tall, overweight women want to look slim, the tall want to lead attention away from their height and thin women strive for a more rounded look.

The following pages illustrate the difference which the right or wrong selection of clothing can make for imperfect figure shapes.

SHORT – WRONG

Padded shoulders and wide lapels accentuate angular cut of suit and create horizontal lines

Wide sleeves make arms look shorter

Jacket too long for this skirt length

Gathered skirt adds fullness and width

Dark suit and light panty-hose "cut" legs, creating a squat look

SHORT – RIGHT

Soft design of shoulders and overblouse creates more fluid lines

Diagonal line across bodice lengthens torso

One-piece, straight-cut dress with slight diagonal at hem elongates the body

Pantyhose and shoes in same color accentuate vertical line

SHORT

Small women seem to shrink in large prints, horizontal stripes, outfits with wide belts and shirts with large cuffs. However, they can walk tall in vertical stripes, one-piece jumpsuits, wrap-around dresses and short jackets.

TALL

Tall women should avoid tiny prints, three-quarter sleeves, tiny earrings and dainty jewelry. They can minimize their height by wearing large coats, sweeping capes and pleated pants or pants with wide legs.

TALL – WRONG

TALL – RIGHT

Dark blouse with high neck makes neck appear longer

High-cut shoulders make arms appear longer

Blouse gives a short-waisted, long-legged look

Vertical stripes elongate the body

Long skirt adds height to body

Pantyhose in same color as shoes create long-legged look

Layered clothes (light-colored blouse, scarf and jacket with wide lapels) add breadth

Full sleeves with cuffs "shorten" arms

Wide belt divides body into more equal proportions

Tucks in skirt add fullness

Skirt just below knees "cuts" long legs

Light-colored pantyhose break monotony and long vertical line of body

HEAVY FIGURE

The heavy-set woman seems to put on weight by wearing clothes with horizontal stripes or large designs, gathered skirts, skirts or dresses with patch pockets at the hips, clinging fabrics, and bulky long-haired furs. She can look slimmer by choosing vertical stripes and patterns, V-neck sweaters, skirts that have a central inverted pleat, outfits in one color only (including pantyhose and shoes), and dress lengths below the knee.

HEAVY – WRONG

Wide cross-collar accentuates a thick neck

Wide cut of bodice adds fullness to waist and hips

Large plaid design creates horizontal line, adding width to body

Shoes with ankle straps make legs look shorter

HEAVY – RIGHT

Detail on shoulder brings the eye "up", creating a longer line

Soft, draping effect of diagonal over-blouse is more flattering

Solid-colored dress is more slenderizing

Longer dress length adds to height and creates a slimmer look

THIN FIGURE

The very thin woman shouldn't wear sleeveless dresses, fabrics with small prints or two-piece dresses (dresses with short jackets). She'll fill out nicely in clothes with horizontal stripes, plaids and patterns; double-breasted suit jackets; skirts with large patch pockets; pleated pants; blouses with yokes, ruffles and gathers and patterned or textured pantyhose in light colors worn with simple, stylish shoes.

THIN – WRONG

Shoulders are "sharp" and shapeless

V-neckline adds length to thin neck

Clinging jersey fabric emphasizes thin shape

Dark, straight dress elongates the body

Below-knee dress length gives "leggy" look

Dark stockings accentuate skinny legs

Thick-soled shoes contrast delicate legs

THIN – RIGHT

Big white collar and puff shoulders of textured sweater give wider look

Light colors give larger, but softer effect

Very full culottes add width

Longer skirt gives legs "shorter" look

Light-colored stockings add fullness

Thin flat heels don't overpower slender legs

Clothes

The way you dress gives people an immediate impression of who you are. Research studies have shown that well-dressed people are judged to be more qualified, more intelligent and more likeable than those who are not. They are treated with respect and are given greater social and business opportunities.

Your appearance can also be the expression of a specific image you want to convey. The right clothes can project an artistic, provocative, authoritative, or demure image; the wrong clothes may indicate neglect, carelessness, or an unawareness of what is appropriate for a certain occasion.

Look through your closet and decide whether or not your clothes reflect the image you want to project. Do they suit your way of life? Do they bring out your most flattering self? If the answer is "no", don't panic! You needn't change your entire wardrobe. Careful planning can result in a closet full of clothes that are functional, versatile and lasting, without resulting in an empty purse.

Selecting colors
We'd like to help you create a wardrobe that is both effective and efficient. The first and easiest method is to choose three colors that go together well. Find your color group in the following pages and note the suggested three-color combinations. Choose one of the combinations and select individual articles of clothing in these colors only. Of course, if you prefer, add a fourth color that goes well with the rest. However, it is not practical to have more than four colors in your wardrobe unless many items are in the "neutral" shades.

Another way to build an effective wardrobe is to start with a neutral color, then add two or three other colors that work well together. For example, taupe works well with purple or black; gray with burgundy and navy. Wardrobe consultants choose one medium-to-dark color and use this for the nucleus, or core, of a client's wardrobe in items like coats, jackets and pants. These clothes are more versatile in solid colors rather than prints. Other shades – accent colors – are added through smaller items such as sweaters, blouses and scarves.

Choosing clothes
The next step is co-ordinating separates. Treat each article of clothing as a separate unit. When you buy a suit, consider it as two separate pieces of clothing, a skirt and a jacket, each of which can be worn with other items. Therefore, the jacket can serve as a blazer worn with your other skirts and pants or over a dress. Choose simple, classic styles with a minimum of detail, as they can be easily interchanged with your other separates.

The third step to a successful wardrobe is choosing clothes for their versatility. Buy clothing that can be worn for several occasions. For example, a shirtwaist dress combined with a blazer can be worn during the day. For evening, try the same dress without the blazer, open the neck to reveal a lacy camisole top and wear high heeled shoes and dressy jewelry.

A suit is very dependable, as it can be worn for many occasions. Light-colored suits require a darker blouse for businesswear; a light-colored blouse looks elegant. The dark suit (navy or black) looks more serious and authoritative than a light one, and is more flexible, as it can be worn for both day and evening. For work, choose a classic white shirt; for evening or theater, a silk shirt, pearl necklace and other dressy jewelry.

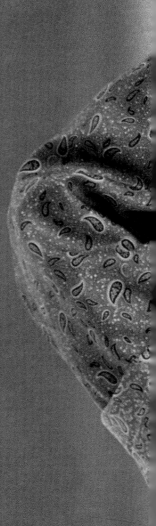

Selecting your clothes

To help you choose clothes and accessories in colors that work well together, we have provided very effective three-color combinations on the following pages and on your individual color chart on the inside front cover. The deeper and darker colors (usually one or two of the three) are more suitable as your core colors in large items like coats, suits, skirts and pants. The lighter and brighter colors should be used as accents for smaller items such as blouses, sweaters, scarves and accessories. By selecting from your three-color combinations and augmenting them with your six neutral colors, you can build a spectacular wardrobe.

Once you have decided on your combination, you can start picking out clothes in the right colors and weeding out any of your existing garments in the wrong colors.

Little by little, move towards the ideal – a wardrobe in which everything matches, from suits to scarves. Even by adding one item a month to a basic suit – be it blouse, beads or belt – you'll soon have a wide variety of changes and need never be heard to complain, "I've nothing to wear".

The three-color combinations we provide here are only a few suggestions for creating a beautiful "working" wardrobe. If you refer to your color chart – and your imagination – the possibilities will be endless!

1

2

3

REDHEADS

Redheads can go wild
with warm colors
like bronze, russet
and terracotta. Earthy
tones of bark, olive
and spice form the
nucleus of your
wardrobe. Corduroy,
tweed and velour
fabrics in brown,
paprika and brick red
are especially becom-
ing to your coloring.

69

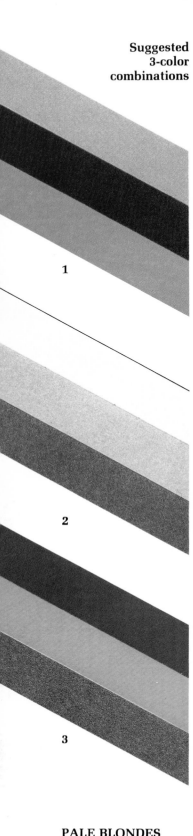

1

2

3

PALE BLONDES
Blondes should think
"soft and subtle"
when co-ordinating
ensembles. Pale
blondes can dream up
a wardrobe based on
such colors as
mushroom, pink,
camel and sand.

Suggested
3-color
combinations

1

2

3

GOLDEN BLONDES
Golden blondes
should substitute
peach or coral for
pink. Natural fabrics
— lightweight wools,
gaberdines, knits,
silks and linens — feel
delightful and look
great in soft colors.

71

Suggested
3-color
combinations

1

2

3

BRUNETTES
Dramatic contrasts of
light and dark set the
stage for a basic
brunette wardrobe.
Make your debut in
black, white, red and
gray, a combination
that's easy to achieve
and always glamor-
ous to wear.

1

2

3

DARK-SKINNED BRUNETTES

Your other three-color combinations are found above, but you're certain to steal the show in black, red and purple. Flannels, crisp cottons, fine wools, silks and satins are your fabrics.

73

Integrating your wardrobe

When you buy a new outfit, experiment with the different looks and combinations you can create by co-ordinating it with existing items in your wardrobe.

Necessities for a flexible wardrobe are: a "basic" suit, a blazer, two shirts (one casual, one silk) and a chemise dress. You can change the look of an old outfit by adding a belt, wearing a vest, or tying two scarves together to co-ordinate with the outfit.

Make a list or drawings of the different clothes items and combina-

tions you have and tape it to the inside of your closet. It is well worth the effort. List whether the outfits are suitable for day or evening.

The clothes you own that are not in "your colors" should be put to one side. If a suit is in your "wrong" color, wear a blouse, vest or scarf in your "right" color that blends well with it. Apply the same principle to your other clothes – your most flattering colors should always be worn close to your face. Gradually eliminate the

CLOTHES	BRUNETTES	DARK-SKINNED BRUNETTES	PALE BLONDES	GOLDEN BLONDES	REDHEADS
suit	navy crepe	black gaberdine	purple & gray tweed	cocoa brown velvet	cream wool
blouse/day	pink (with bow)	taupe	pale pink	cream jaquard	russet
blouse/evening	navy & wine silk paisley print	red silk	gray or purple satin	peach satin	cream silk
cardigan	navy	taupe	gray	cream	terracotta
pullover	navy or wine cable-knit	red wool polo neck	purple & pink mohair crew neck	peach or ivory angora V-neck	teal blue fair isle wool
vest	wine & navy argyle	taupe or black suede	pink or gray wool	sand suede	camel suede
skirt	white or wine & navy tweed	taupe	gray	peach suede	cream
pants	navy	white	taupe	brown	brown & cream tweed
ACCESSORIES					
scarf	pink & burgundy silk paisley	long red & black polka dot	purple & pink paisley	brown print	russet & brown striped
shoes	navy or burgundy	black	gray	brown	camel
handbag/day	navy or burgundy	black	gray	brown	camel or brown
handbag/evening	silver or navy	black or silver	silver or gray	brown or gold	amber or gold
jewelry/day	long strand white pearls	silver chain necklaces & earrings	pink pearls in choker or rope & pearl earrings	amber beads, coral & pearl necklace & earrings	amber or tiger's eye necklace & earrings
jewelry/evening	burgundy or garnet stone earrings	diamanté & silver	diamanté & silver necklace & earrings	gold chain & earrings	gold necklace & earrings

wrong-colored clothes. Make a list of what you own and another of what you need.

Investing in your wardrobe

Decide just how much money you want to invest in your wardrobe and plan a budget. What items do you need the most for your lifestyle – sportswear? work clothes? evening wear?

The clothes worn most often are: coat, blazer, suit, skirts and pants. Choose them carefully. Pick fabrics that are seasonless – silks, silk-like synthetics, crepes, wools or jersey knits, and choose neutral colors, as these are more wearable. Update these clothes later on by adding inexpensive accessories in the newest fashion color (if it is in your color category).

Before buying, ask yourself: Do I need it? Is it in my color scheme? Does it go with the other things in my wardrobe? Does it suit my body shape?

Shopping hints

● Shop early in the season when there is a wide selection of clothing from which to choose.
● Pick a good time to shop. The best time is when you are not rushed. Department stores are usually less crowded in the morning and early in the week.
● Be selective. It is not how much you spend but how well you choose.
● Save time by finding a store that sells the type of clothing you like.
● Make a note of the designers' labels when you find clothes that fit well. Look for those names when you shop.
● Dark clothes are the most practical, as you can wear them for day and for evening. But, in warm weather wear lighter, more colorful clothes or neutrals and whites or cream.
● Invest in natural fiber fabrics (silks, as silks, cottons, linens and wools) because they wear well and always look attractive.
● Avoid spur-of-the-moment buying. Don't get carried away by a sale. Stick to your shopping list.

Organizing your wardrobe

Organize your closet to make it functional. Most closets are cluttered with clothes that are no longer serviceable. If you have not worn an article of clothing for two years, eliminate it from your closet. The chances are that you will never wear it again.

Go through the clothes that are too small for you and store them. Check the clothes that have to be cleaned and mended. Never keep anything in your closet that is not wearable.

Hang similar items together. Put your suit jacket with your other jackets and the suit skirt with the other skirts; they will be used as co-ordinates to combine with your other separates. Hang your clothing according to color, starting with the whites and going on to the darker colors. Check to see that everything is hanging straight. Use only one kind of hanger to give a uniform look to your clothes. You can use plastic, wood or padded hangers.

Try to avoid hanging one garment over the other, as it makes it more difficult to find what you need. If you are short of space, invest in space savers such as multiple blouse, skirt and pants hangers which hold up to six pieces each.

Storage tips

● Put knit items in shelves, drawers or boxes as they stretch out of shape if hung up
● Hang easily-tangled chains from a tie bar
● Hang the belts you wear most often on a coat hook. Put the rest in plastic boxes
● Furs, leathers and silks need to breathe and cannot be stored in plastic bags
● Use multiple hangers to store pants, shirts and skirts.
● Use wire hangers carefully, as they may distort delicate garments.
● Use sachets or empty perfume vials in your lingerie drawer to keep your clothing fragrant

Accessories

Besides using accessories like belts, shoes and handbags for their obvious functional purposes, use them to complete your total look.

Handbags
A handbag is your most important accessory. Buy the best you can afford, preferably leather; it is well worth the price for the many years of good wear it will give you. A matching wallet and a gold or silver pen give an especially smart look. Your basic wardrobe should include three handbags, two for day and one that can be worn for day or evening. Choose from your neutral colors, and if possible, match your bag with your shoe color. If it does not match the shoes, the bag should be a lighter color.

Belts
Belts are a high-fashion item. They tie together a skirt-and-blouse look and give a wonderful accent to an outfit. The 1½″–2″ belt is a good basic investment, especially if it is in snake or lizard skin. Two thin belts worn together can create the look of a wide belt. The purchase of a new belt can give a "this year" look to more than one outfit. But remember that belt styles date more quickly than other accessories, so do not expect a fantasy style to carry you through many seasons.

Shoes
Choose a neutral color that will work with all your clothes. Light neutrals are best for warm climates and for summer; dark neutrals for cool climates and for winter. If you choose a shoe color that is not in your neutral category, make sure the color is the same shade, or darker, than your outfit. Snakeskin, suede and patent leather can be worn both day and evening. Silk shoes are for evening only, or for formal wear, as are silver and gold. Pumps or small heels are for business and day wear; flat sandals are for leisure wear.

Hats
Hats needn't be worn for special occasions only, but make sure that the style and color you choose goes with your outfit. For instance, a boater style hat goes well with either a simple suit or a dress with a sailor collar. Check that the size is in proportion to your height and body shape.

Jewelry
Your best investment is your watch. For a neat look, a leather strap is a good choice – black for brunettes, tan for blondes and brown for redheads. A simple, delicate chain bracelet worn with your watch looks stylish.

Regarding rings, simple is best for daytime. An intertwining ring on your small finger can be very fashionable. However, unless it is an engagement ring, a ring set with stones is better worn for evening.

Classic designs for earrings are round, knot, or geometric shapes for daytime wear. Drop earrings and stone settings should be worn in the evening. For fun, try diamanté or crystal with dark-colored casual clothes for daytime. Colorful plastics are best with sportswear.

A useful necklace for day wear is a simple gold or silver chain worn close to the neck. The 16″-long necklace is the right length for an open shirt; the 24″ pendant is a good slenderizer, as it gives an elongated effect. Of course, pearl necklaces (and earrings) never go out of style.

BRUNETTES
Lavish yourself with evening accessories that out-shine the stars. All brunettes sparkle in silver — that icy color so tantalizing against dark hair or dark skin. Wear it on belts, shoes and handbags, or in jewelry with pearls and diamonds.

REDHEADS
A casual but dressed-up feeling can easily be yours with accessories in varying textures. Soft suedes, felts and leathers are widely available in your mellow tones from coppery-gold to deep chocolate-brown. Red or yellow gold jewelry brings a warmth to the redhead's looks.

BLONDES
Blondes blossom in the warm tones of both red and yellow gold, so choose them for your jewelry. For rich elegance in either daytime or nighttime wear leather shoes, belts and handbags in your most useful color.

Tying it all together

Just a single accessory can change the whole look of an ensemble. Wearing a silk cravat under a plain shirt gives you a "dressed up" appearance; the addition of a scarf worn fan-style enables you to wear the same dress at night that you wore all day. If you tend to fumble rather than fix a scarf into the shape you want, here are some simple instructions for different styles.

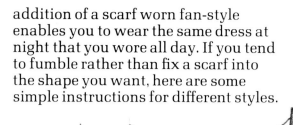

LOOP ▶
Fold a long scarf in half lengthwise, then fold again, bringing top and bottom ends together. Place around neck.

Thread loose ends through loop and pull to the desired length.

Note: This can be worn close to the neck or loosely tied in a casual look. The loop is especially effective on a man's silk paisley or checked scarf.

◀ FAN
Open a square scarf. Gather together each end until the whole scarf is pleated. Hold ends firmly and place around neck. Pin or knot two sides together close to neck. (Scarf should flare out in a fan shape.) Wear fan to the side.

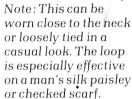

CRAVAT ▶
Open a square scarf. Pick up the center of the scarf and tie a knot.

Open scarf with the knot side down (knot is concealed). Take two corners of the scarf and tie around your neck.

Insert bottom of scarf into V-neck sweater or shirt. Fasten to undergarment to hold securely, if you prefer.

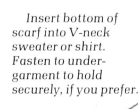

THE EXECUTIVE

The look:
Confident, capable dynamic

Hair:
Orderly, well-groomed

Cosmetics:
Cream-based foundation to give a smooth, polished look; cream or powder highlighter on brow bone and cheeks for emphasis; light application of eye shadow; any but the very harsh or bright colored lipsticks

Wardrobe:
Quality clothing that can be mixed and matched into many changes: suits, skirts, blouses, blazers. Shoes and handbags to match suits

Jewelry
A watch with a leather strap; classic earrings; stick-pin; pearls; small rings, preferably with small stones or no stones at all

Fragrance:
Refreshing scents (mandarin, orange, lime) with touches of magnolia or cinnamon; for evening, woodsy, herb or moss-based blends

What to avoid:
Low-cut or sheer blouses, glittery fabrics, clinging clothes

Tips:
Keep a make-up case in your desk for freshening up; carry a spare pair of pantyhose in your briefcase in case of a tear, or to wear for evening

Changing images

The clothes and accessories you wear not only reflect your moods, but reveal something about the life you lead. They can also be the tools for creating the images you want to convey. Whatever situation you are in – be it a business meeting or a cocktail party, there are specific clothes, cosmetics and accessories you can wear to look terrific.

Over the next few pages we show a variety of looks which take into account the kind of life women lead today. Here, you will find the techniques for successful dressing for both work and leisure occasions. We hope, too, that our techniques will be adapted to suit women of many ages.

It's never too late to change, or reinforce, your image. All it takes is attention to detail and a certain amount of "dress sense". Armed with the information found within this book, and your individual colour guidelines, a new you is well within your grasp.

The look:
Efficient, energetic, imaginative

Hair:
A good cut that's easy to manage

Wardrobe:
Mainly mix-and-match separates —
skirts, sweaters and blouses. For a practical look, wear monochromatic schemes with clothes in different textures

Cosmetics:
Shouldn't be too harsh or too heavy.
Bright-colored lipstick shouldn't be applied too thickly.
Eye shadows should be well-blended, and eye liner not too severe

Jewelry
Simple watch, rings, and necklaces.
Costume jewelry is fine, but keep it small

Fragrance:
Flowery scents —
sandalwood, orange blossom and lilac

What to avoid:
Too many colors in one outfit — three co-ordinating colors in clothing and access-ories should be the limit. Also avoid sparkling jewelry, outlandish hairstyles, and gold and glittery eye and lip make-up

Tips:
Solid-colored blouses, especially light colors rather than prints, provide more versatility

THE AFTER FIVE LOOK

The look:
Smooth and
sophisticated

Hair:
Tousled or sleek, but
well-styled.

Cosmetics:
Heavier eye make-up
than for daytime, but
subtly blended, with
graduated colors
(pink, purple and
violet, for example)
and glistening high-
lighter in silver, gold
or peachy-pink
lipstick should be a
shade darker than
daytime color

Wardrobe:
Skirts in silk, taffeta,
or crepe with match-
ing or contrasting
blouses in silk or
satin; velvet or
brocaded jackets;
dresses in brocade or
silk

Jewelry
Three-stranded pearl
choker with cameo
or diamanté clasps;
heavy chain necklace
with a big artificial or
real diamond
pendant; diamond
studded earrings,
emeralds, rubies,
sapphires

Fragrance:
Spicy scents
(cinnamon, ginger,
clove) or oriental
blends (musk, civet)
in heady, lingering
aromas

What to avoid:
Too much jewelry or
lots of different-
colored stones in
one piece

Tips:
Invest in an expensive
evening bag and
wrap, like a velvet
cape

THE AGE OF EXPERIENCE

The look:
Graceful, dignified, personable

Hair:
Soft-looking, swept off the face, never longer than shoulder-length

Cosmetics:
Sheer foundation; softer lipstick and blusher colors; avoid harsh or silvery colors on eyes

Wardrobe:
Tailored, classic styles; unmatched suits, short-style jackets and blouses with slightly-puffed sleeves that give a youthful look

Jewelry:
Bulky or geometric-shaped earrings can improve the less-than-perfect jawline. Pearls and beads inter-twined create a luxurious look

Fragrance:
Fresh floral scents (rose, gardenia, jasmine) and fruity scents (lemon, lime)

What to avoid:
Dull mousey colors, long dangling ear-rings which tend to pull the face down-ward, very blue or purple lipstick. Don't wait too long to retouch hair color if you have colored your gray hair

Tips:
Wear soft fabrics in unconstructed jackets, and soft, crushy belts; wear collars open. Pay attention to your posture and grooming to retain a young attitude

The new you

Maybe you don't have the ideal figure or the perfect proportions to make you look great in absolutely anything you wear, or maybe you're tired of the same style clothes or hairdo you've worn for the past four or five years. Perhaps you want to change your image and let the world see a new side to your personality. Anything is possible if you choose your clothes and cosmetics carefully, select a becoming hairstyle and wear a smile!

This busy mother of five has a part-time job in the evenings. She has little time to devote to applying cosmetics or shopping for clothes. She is 5´ 7″ tall and wears a size 16 dress.

We have chosen a very practical suit for her in hard-wearing corduroy. A shocking pink blouse and scarf provide a wonderful accent to her attractive dark coloring. Her eyes were colored with soft pink and violet eye shadows, and her lipstick and blusher are in fuchsia tones. Her hair was permed and restyled into an easy-to-manage bob.

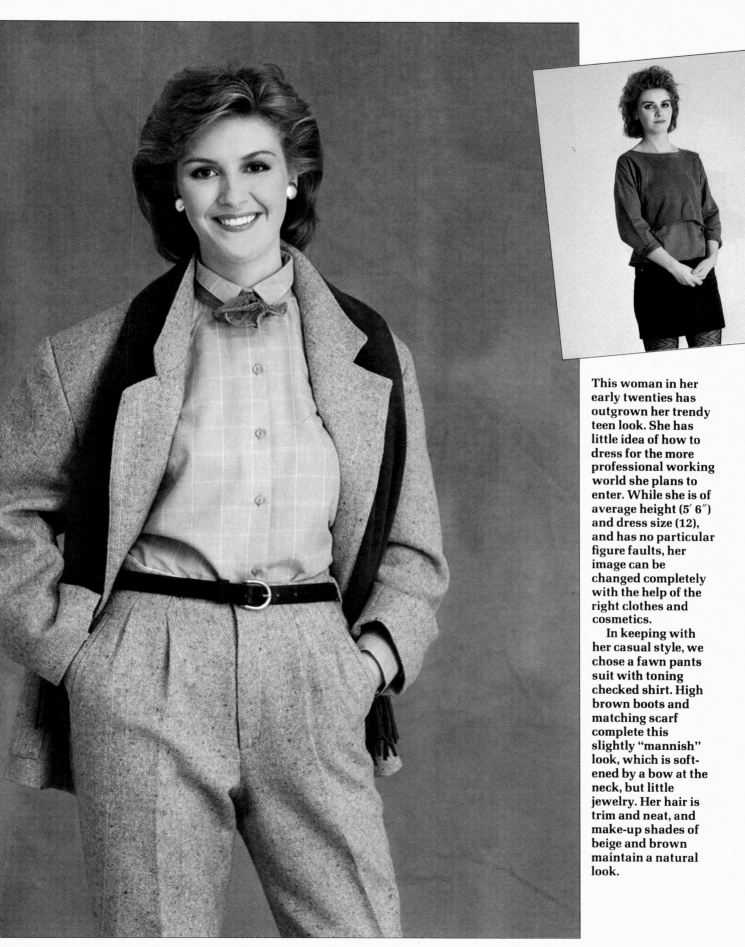

This woman in her early twenties has outgrown her trendy teen look. She has little idea of how to dress for the more professional working world she plans to enter. While she is of average height (5′ 6″) and dress size (12), and has no particular figure faults, her image can be changed completely with the help of the right clothes and cosmetics.

In keeping with her casual style, we chose a fawn pants suit with toning checked shirt. High brown boots and matching scarf complete this slightly "mannish" look, which is softened by a bow at the neck, but little jewelry. Her hair is trim and neat, and make-up shades of beige and brown maintain a natural look.

This young grand-mother has not really changed her image since she was a "hippie" in the 1960s. Today her look is neither fashionable nor flattering. She is 4′ 11″ tall, wears a large dress size, and is short-waisted.

She looks taller and slimmer in her pleated camel skirt and long vest which camouflage her short waist and slims her hips. The checked scarf also draws the eye down-ward creating the illusion of height which is so important for petite women; and worn with its matching hat, makes a smart finish to this classic ensemble. Her hair has been cut shorter and swept off her face to give a more youthful appearance. A warm peach foundation, coral lipstick and teal blue eye shadow all contribute to her new, more contem-porary look.

This older, petite woman, just under 5 foot, is overweight (wears a size 20 dress) and has a large bust. She also has a full face with a double chin and wears little make-up.

A crepe dress with box pleats was chosen for her as it creates a long line, thus adding height to her figure. Long strands of pearls echo the vertical line; a matching hat adds softness and elegance.

Her hair was lightened to an ash gray-blonde and styled off her face in an "upswept" wave. Cosmetics were applied subtly – concealer under the eyes eliminates puffiness; contouring with rose-brown blush reshapes her full cheeks; teal blue eye color and pink-mauve lipstick and blusher contribute to the overall softness of her new face.

Travel

Travelling can be a nightmare if you are over-burdened with heavy suit-cases. However, with your new color and clothes know-how, you can travel with the minimum of luggage and the maximum of changes.

Choose two co-ordinating colors from your scheme (or several shades of one color) and select clothes in these colors that are both practical and versatile. If you are a brunette, we recommend either a black-and-red or a taupe-and-purple color combination. A pale blonde might like french blue and burgundy or ice pink and off-white with the color accent in a navy scarf. Golden blondes look nice in camel and gray or Mediterranean blue and daffodil yellow. Cinnamon and dark chocolate or brick red and cream are winning combinations for the auburn redhead.

By mixing and matching individual articles, you can create a closet with enough variety to last your entire trip, be it three days or three weeks. Below are suggestions for the minimum number of clothes to take on two city trips – one is for five days, the other for four weeks.

The woman on the facing page is taking a four-week trip. Overleaf are twelve additional outfits that she can put together with our simple formula.

What to pack for a five-day city trip:

1 suit
1 skirt
1 pr. pants
2 blouses (1 day, 1 evening)
1 sweater
1 scarf
1 coat
hat (optional)
2 prs. shoes
2 handbags (1 day, 1 evening)
1 nightgown, bathrobe, folding
  slippers
3 prs. pantyhose
3 sets underwear
1 slip
jewelry

What to pack for a four-week city trip:

2 suits
1 skirt
2 prs. pants
5 blouses (3 day, 2 evening)
3 sweaters (1 cardigan, 2 pullovers)
1 vest
2 scarves
1 coat
hat (optional)
2 prs. shoes
2 handbags (1 day, 1 evening)
2 nightgowns, bathrobe, folding
  slippers
5 prs. pantyhose
5 sets underwear
1 slip
jewelry

Note: Don't forget your cosmetic bag and hair-dryer!

Stepping out Ten o'clock meeting, luncheon at one, three o'clock appointment, drinks at five, dinner at eight, dancing 'til ? . . . Whatever the schedule or the occasion, the fashion-conscious woman will travel right – and light – by color-co-ordinating her clothes and packing the most versatile items. More than

thirty changes of clothes are possible in our four-week trip, twelve of which are shown above. The two suits are in light and dark shades of one color, but they needn't be – just pick colors that will match everything else. With a different look everyday, you'll never be bored with your clothes!

Acknowledgments

Dorling Kindersley would like to thank the following people for their help in producing this book:

Illustrators
Shari Peacock, Lynne Robinson

Photography for cover and page 56
Colin Thomas

Stylist
Liz E. London

Make-up Artists
Peter Coburn, Keiko Eno, Audrey Maxwell, Miguel Mendoza, Helen Robertson

Hair Stylists
Gregory Cazaly and Paula Mann from Joshua Galvin Hair Salon, Margaret Friel from Trevor Sorbie

Reproduction
Reprocolor International

Typesetters
Chambers Wallace

Elizabeth Arden

to whom we are extremely grateful for their extensive help in providing cosmetics, which were used throughout the book

ANGLIA TELEVISION
who kindly gave permission to reproduce the "before" pictures (pages 88, 90 and 91) from their ABOUT ANGLIA feature "The New You"

Alexon, Aquascutum of London Limited, Castleberry Knits, Dickins and Jones, Fenn Wright and Manson Ltd., Harrods, Hobbs, I Blues, Shoes by Charles Jourdan, Soo Yung Lee, Lumiere, Adrien Mann Jewelry, Mansfield Originals Ltd., Next, Harvey Nichols, Albert Nipon, Ports of Bond Street International Ltd., Selfridges, Miss Selfridge, David Shilling (hats on pp. 40 and 77), Gianni Versace, Viva, Wallis, Fashion Fair Beauty Products and Kanebo Cosmetics